THE LIVING GOSPEL

Daily Devotions for Lent 2016

Charles Paolino

Ave Maria Press AVE Notre Dame, Indiana

Charles Paolino is associate editor at RENEW International. He is a permanent deacon of the Diocese of Metuchen, New Jersey, ministering in liturgy, preaching, and adult education at Our Lady of Lourdes Church in Whitehouse Station. He also is a columnist for *The Catholic Spirit*, the newspaper and website of the Diocese of Metuchen, and a freelance theater critic.

Paolino spent forty-three years in newspaper journalism and more than thirty years as an adjunct instructor of English at various universities and colleges, including Seton Hall and Rutgers. He earned a bachelor's degree in communications from Seton Hall and a master's degree in journalism from Penn State. He and his wife, Patricia Ann, live in Whitehouse Station. They have four grown children and five grandchildren.

Excerpts from the *Lectionary for Mass for Use in the Dioceses of the United States of America, second typical edition* © 2001, 1998, 1997, 1986, 1970 Confraternity of Christian Doctrine, Inc., Washington, DC. Used with permission. All rights reserved. No portion of this text may be reproduced by any means without permission in writing from the copyright owner.

© 2015 by Charles Paolino

All rights reserved. No part of this book may be used or reproduced in any manner whatsoever, except in the case of reprints in the context of reviews, without written permission from Ave Maria Press ®, Inc., P.O. Box 428, Notre Dame, IN 46556, 1-800-282-1865.

Founded in 1865, Ave Maria Press is a ministry of the United States Province of Holy Cross.

www.avemariapress.com

Paperback: ISBN-13 978-1-59471-644-7

E-book: ISBN-13 978-1-59471-645-4

Cover image "At the Foot of the Cross" ©2012 by Jeni Butler, artworkbyjeni.wix.com.

Cover and text design by John Carson.

Printed and bound in the United States of America.

INTRODUCTION

> Even the angels that Jacob saw in a dream were not
> flying but climbing one step at a time.
>
> ~*Pope John Paul I*
> *Discourse to the clergy of Rome*
> *September 7, 1978*

The September Pope, as John Paul I is known, gave
the clergy of Rome some advice about what he called
"the great discipline," in which the soul strives contin-
uously to overcome its weaknesses "and to acquire, a
little at a time, the habit of judging and behaving in
all the circumstances of life according to the maxims
of the Gospel and the examples of Jesus." The soul
achieves this, the pope emphasized, "a little at a time,"
just as the angels in Jacob's dream climbed the ladder
to heaven step by step (Gn 28:12).

This gradual ascent is the focus of our attention
during the season of Lent, when we find time and
space amid the demands and distractions of everyday existence to examine our lives and re-form them
in ways that move us closer to God.

We don't make this climb all at once, we don't
make it only during Lent, and we don't make it without experiencing some lapses and reversals along the
way. What matters is that we continue, relying on the
patience and mercy of God.

The goal we strive for in this ascent is, as John
Paul I said, a life that is ordered according to the teachings and example of Jesus—and that means according
to the great commandments: love of God and love of

neighbor. Working on our relationship with God is inextricably bound up with working on our relationship with the human family.

Throughout the gospels, Jesus both preaches and practices self-giving—not only in his overt acts of compassion but also in his view of himself as the servant of all. It is a high standard, but it is the example Jesus set and the example he called on us to imitate. Acts of self-denial and acts of charity can help us see ourselves not as the center of all that is but as members of a world much larger than ourselves.

This book of reflections is an invitation for you to spend a small part of each day focusing on your interior life. For each day of Lent, there are prompts for prayer, including a passage from the Psalm or Old Testament reading of that day's Mass, a few verses from the gospel reading for that day, a personal reflection that draws on the lesson of that gospel passage, a suggested step toward spiritual growth, and a closing prayer. There are also gospel passages, short reflections, and prayers for the Easter Triduum—Holy Thursday, Good Friday, and Holy Saturday.

You may benefit most from this book if you devote about ten minutes to each day's reflection. Committing to the same time of day and the same quiet place can help you establish a rhythm for this part of your Lenten observance. You may spend the time as you wish. You might, for example, choose to read the entire gospel reading for each day instead of only the shortened passages printed for each day. What's important is that in spending time with this book you move closer to God "a little at a time" with Jesus as your companion every step of the way.

For one believes with the heart and so is justified, and one confesses with the mouth and so is saved. For the scripture says, "No one who believes in him will be put to shame." For there is no distinction between Jew and Greek; the same Lord is Lord of all, enriching all who call upon him. For "everyone who calls on the name of the Lord will be saved."

~Romans 10:10–13, NABRE

February 10
Ash Wednesday

Spend a minute or two in silence. Set aside whatever might hinder your prayer.

Give me back the joy of your salvation, and a willing spirit sustain in me.

~Psalm 51:14

Read Matthew 6:1–6, 16–18.

"When you fast, anoint your head and wash your face, so that you may not appear to be fasting, except to your Father who is hidden. And your Father who sees what is hidden will repay you."

~Matthew 6:17–18

Fast with a Purpose

I grew up under "the old system." In the 1940s and '50s, the Lenten fast still ended at noon on Holy Saturday. For me, it was the lifting of a great burden because my family had a grocery store where I had easy access to candy, ice cream, and soda. But when Ash Wednesday arrived, I was cut off. So on Holy Saturday, I was sure to be in the store by 11:45, watching the clock while both hands crept toward noon.

I scrupulously observed the fast, although I could have snitched a candy bar or a Popsicle when the store was closed and my parents were distracted. There was no heroism in this; I observed the fast—and went to confession on Saturday and Mass on Sunday—because I was afraid not to. When the fast was over, I felt the way athletes must feel when they have completed a triathlon.

In the decades since then, I have learned that fasting is not an ordeal to test our resolve, punishment for our sins, or self-denial that prepares us to better enjoy self-indulgence. I have learned that rather than delivering us safe and sound to our routine, Lent should unsettle us in a way that lasts long after the clock strikes twelve.

As Pope Francis has explained, fasting makes sense only if it fine-tunes our awareness of the material and spiritual poverty in which so many live and heightens our motivation to use wisely and share the resources God has given us.

The holy mark we receive today will fade, but we can resolve as we receive it not to be content so long as a brother or sister is cold or hungry.

ACT

I will make an account of my resources—time, talent, skills, funds, and material goods—and honestly consider what part of these I could reasonably share with someone in need.

PRAY

Generous God, we thank you for all that you have given us. May the fast and prayer of this holy season help us value your gifts—not only as blessings in our own lives but also as resources that we can share with those who are in need who are our sisters and brothers. We ask this through Jesus Christ, our Lord. Amen.

FEBRUARY 11
THURSDAY AFTER ASH WEDNESDAY

BEGIN

Spend a minute or two in silence. Set aside whatever might hinder your prayer.

PRAY

I have set before you life and death, the blessing and the curse. Choose life, then, that you and your descendants may live.

~*Deuteronomy 30:19*

LISTEN

Read Luke 9:22–25.

"For whoever wishes to save his life will lose it, but whoever loses his life for my sake will save it."

~*Luke 9:24*

No Effort Is Wasted

One of my college books included a passage written by the British author W. Somerset Maugham. "To myself," Maugham wrote, "I am the most important person in the world . . . but from the standpoint of common sense, I am of no consequence whatever. It would have made small difference to the universe if I had never existed." That passage made me realize that, at times, I too saw the world as revolving around me—an illusion shared by hundreds of millions of human beings.

Deny your very self, Jesus says, and doing that may begin with recognizing that no one person is the center of all that is. But that shouldn't lead anyone to the conclusion that he or she is "of no consequence whatever." On the contrary, the self-denial that Jesus calls us to is the first step toward committing all of our gifts not to our own comfort, influence, or social standing but to the well-being of our closest neighbors and of the world at large.

Regardless of its problems, the world is a far better place because of the unselfish actions of countless people who lost their lives, as Jesus meant it, rather than saving them—who gave away parts of their lives in order to bless the lives of others. The fact that most of those selfless people are anonymous and perhaps soon forgotten does not reduce their importance, individually and collectively, to life on earth.

As Pope Francis has written, "No single act of love for God will be lost, no generous effort is meaningless."

ACT

I will spend time today recalling the gifts and favors large and small with which others have blessed me and made my life better. I will pray in gratitude for the gift givers and their gifts, and I will pray for the will to bless others in the same way.

PRAY

Lord Jesus Christ, help me to imitate your life, not focusing on myself but freely devoting my energies and resources to building up the lives of others. Amen.

FEBRUARY 12
FRIDAY AFTER ASH WEDNESDAY

BEGIN

Spend a minute or two in silence. Set aside whatever might hinder your prayer.

PRAY

My sacrifice, O God, is a contrite spirit; a heart contrite and humbled, O God, you will not spurn.

~Psalm 51:19

LISTEN

Read Matthew 9:14–15.

Jesus answered them, "Can the wedding guests mourn as long as the bridegroom is with them?"

~Matthew 9:15a

Then They Will Fast

When the playwright-director George Abbott was 106 years old, he attended the opening of a Broadway revival of *Damn Yankees*, for which he had written the book forty years before. As Abbott walked down the aisle, the audience stood and applauded, and Abbott said to his companion, "There must be someone important here." There was, indeed. The audience knew it, and the audience celebrated.

Unlike that astute audience, the folks we read about in today's gospel passage missed out on an even bigger reason to celebrate: the presence of Jesus among them. Not only did they fail to recognize him as the long-awaited messiah but they also failed to accept even the truth of his message of unconditional compassion and love.

Referring to himself as the bridegroom, Jesus said that those who walked with him and learned from him had reason to rejoice. But he was also preparing them for the time when he would no longer be physically present among them and they would be left to live as he had taught them and spread his Gospel. Then they would fast, and now we fast—through prayer, penance, self-denial, and charity. Through our fasting we put aside both the distractions of a wasteful and noisy world and the preoccupation with our own comfort and convenience. Through our fasting we remember how much he sacrificed to overcome the consequences of sin and death and to offer the hope of eternal life. Through our fasting we see more clearly our mission as his disciples: to be his presence in the lives of so many who need sustenance, solace, and healing.

ACT

I will pray about how I am capable of making Jesus present in the lives of others, especially those whom I find unappealing or with whom I have differences.

PRAY

Lord Jesus, help me to clearly see during Lent and throughout the year how I may make you present to the least of my brothers and sisters, treating them as you would treat them, so that they, too, can celebrate your promise of salvation and eternal life. Amen.

FEBRUARY 13

SATURDAY AFTER ASH WEDNESDAY

BEGIN

Spend a minute or two in silence. Set aside whatever may hinder your prayer.

PRAY

For you, O LORD, are good and forgiving, abounding in kindness to all who call upon you.

~Psalm 86:5

LISTEN

Read Luke 5:27–32.

"Those who are healthy do not need a physician, but the sick do. I have not come to call the righteous to repentance but sinners."

~Luke 5:31–32

Our Healer Is Always at Hand

One of the personalities in the cast of characters of my childhood had the quaint name of Dr. Owsley Duncan. Dr. Duncan was, in effect, the primary-care physician for my grandparents; when I was a boy, he seemed to me to be ancient. He lived in a Victorian house in a city adjacent to my hometown and kept his money in a chamois bag in the bottom drawer of an oak roll-top desk.

Like many doctors five and six decades ago, Dr. Duncan made house calls. He didn't drive, so he took a bus from his street to ours—a distance of about four miles. He did what Jesus said a physician did: he went where he was needed.

In that sense, Dr. Duncan himself was a metaphor for Jesus, who went out of his way to encounter people who needed healing, the folks often summed up by the Pharisees as "tax collectors and sinners." That was the great gift that Jesus gave to the people of his time and still gives to us: that when our spirits are ailing or in pain, he does not wait passively for us to seek him out but makes himself available to us in the sacraments, in the gospels, and in the intimacy of prayer.

For that reason, we can undertake our Lenten practices with confidence that Jesus Christ will not be watching from a distance but will be present as we pray, as we fast, and as we perform acts of charity and justice, and he will touch us with the grace that only he can give.

ACT

I will spend some quiet time each day this week considering one way in which I would like to live more in tune with the Gospel and opening my heart and mind to the healing touch of Jesus.

PRAY

Lord Jesus, you went out to bless those who acknowledged their failings, and you invited them to follow you. Help me to see the ways in which I need your help in order to be a more faithful disciple. Amen.

SUNDAY, FEBRUARY 14
FIRST WEEK OF LENT

BEGIN

Spend a minute or two in silence. Set aside anything that might hinder your prayer.

PRAY

Because he clings to me, I will deliver him; I will set him on high because he acknowledges my name.

~Psalm 91:14

LISTEN

Read Luke 4:1–13.

"It is written: *You shall worship the Lord, your God, and him alone shall you serve.*"

~Luke 4:8b

All that Glitters Is Not Gold

When brothers Bill and Bud Havens made the 1924 US Olympic canoeing team, Bill was favored to win a gold medal. But Bill learned that his wife was likely to deliver their second child while he was in France, so he gave up his place on the team. Bill's sons—Frank, who was born during the '24 games, and Bill Jr.—also became paddlers, and Frank won a silver medal in the 1948 Olympics. Then, in 1952, Frank won the 10,000-meter singles event in Helsinki and sent his dad this telegram: "Thanks for waiting around for me to get born. . . . I'm coming home with the gold medal you should have won." It was a fitting reward for Bill Havens's choice between basking in personal glory and fulfilling his role as husband and parent.

Today's gospel passage is also about choices. Three times the devil cajoled Jesus to act out of an exalted sense of self; three times Jesus refused by declaring that God, not the self, is paramount in human life. This episode was a reversal of the choice made by Adam and Eve, who put their ambition and their will above the will of God and, in effect, made themselves gods.

How do our everyday choices compare to the choice made by Adam and Eve and the choices made by Jesus? Whether it's something simple, such as either yielding in traffic or cutting someone off, or something complex, such as either turning in an accurate expense account or cheating an employer, whose will wins out—ours or God's?

ACT

I will reflect on my choices and pray in thanksgiving for God's guidance when I have acted rightly and in repentance for any mistakes I have made.

PRAY

O God, you have given us, alone among your earthly creatures, the gift of free will. May your Holy Spirit always guide us when we use that gift so that our choices may first serve you and, in your name, the general welfare of our brothers and sisters in this world. Amen.

Monday, February 15
First Week of Lent

BEGIN

Spend a minute or two in silence. Set aside whatever might hinder your prayer.

PRAY

You shall love your neighbor as yourself. I am the LORD.

~Leviticus 19:18b

LISTEN

Read Matthew 25:31–46.

"Amen, I say to you, whatever you did for one of these least brothers of mine, you did for me."

~Matthew 25:40b

"Come, You Who Are Blessed"

When my mother was in her seventies, she surprised us by enrolling as a "foster grandmother" at a center for mentally challenged people. Foster grandmothers helped the staff care for the youngest residents, and Mom worked with the babies in the nursery.

Mom had been a homemaker for most of her adult life and then worked in the office of a company that serviced book publishers; she had never come in direct contact with mentally challenged people. And yet this new experience gave her some of the greatest joy of her life. She loved to tell us about the children (who sometimes kicked her and vomited on her); she showed us pictures of them, cheerfully described their antics, and called them her "little angels." Mom, a woman of faith, didn't seem to think she was doing these children a favor; she simply extended to them the same generosity she had been extending to family, friends, and strangers throughout her life. On the day of judgment described by Jesus in the Gospel of Matthew, Mom might be among those who ask the Son of Man, "When did we see you in need and care for you?"

The Gospel implies that we all are called to cultivate in ourselves that same frame of mind, caring for those in need—not out of a sense of obligation, not out of a desire for praise or reward, but out of a conviction that all human beings, no matter how distinguished by want, illness, or disability, share the humanity of Jesus himself. To love them is to love him.

ACT

I will consider this question: who are the "least" of Jesus' brothers and sisters in my parish or community, and what is my relationship with them?

PRAY

Lord Jesus, through your incarnation you became the brother of us all, the living embodiment of the love God has for his people. Help me to be a reflection of that love by embracing all people, without distinction, as my brothers and sisters. Amen.

TUESDAY, FEBRUARY 16
FIRST WEEK OF LENT

BEGIN

Spend a minute or two in silence. Set aside anything that might hinder your prayer.

PRAY

The LORD has eyes for the just, and ears for their cry.

~Psalm 34:16

LISTEN

Read Matthew 6:7–15.

"If you forgive men their transgressions, your heavenly Father will forgive you. But if you do not forgive men, neither will your Father forgive your transgressions."

~Matthew 6:14–15

"As We Forgive Those . . ."

In both my parish ministry and in my profession, I have spent a lot of time talking with adults about the gospels. Something I hear repeatedly is that adults find forgiveness to be one of the most challenging aspects of our Christian faith. Many folks find it hard to accept the idea that God will unconditionally forgive their sins; even more find it hard to unconditionally extend their own forgiveness. This last applies both to those who have offended or hurt them personally and to those who have offended their sense of justice, such as brutal dictators, terrorists, or other violent criminals.

Accepting what Jesus meant when he taught us to "forgive those who trespass against us" begins with accepting the fact that God is not only willing but also eager to forgive us when we turn back to him, that God holds out forgiveness not as a kind of bait to prompt us to behave in a certain way but rather as a gift he wants to give us. That is how Jesus expects us to forgive even those who may seem to us to be beyond the reach of God's grace and therefore our compassion. It is a radical idea—forgiving even the worst offenders—but it is what Jesus taught and what Jesus himself did, even as he was dying on the Cross.

ACT

I will reflect on whom I find most difficult to forgive, and I will commit myself in prayer to let go of my anger and commend such people to God's judgment and mercy. I will try to remember that, just as Jesus shared in human nature, I share with Jesus an unlimited capacity to forgive.

PRAY

Lord Jesus, as you suffered on the Cross you asked your Father to forgive those who were unjustly putting you to death. Following your example, I ask forgiveness for all who have offended or harmed me in any way and forgiveness for the times when I have harbored resentment or anger toward others. May God have mercy on us all. Amen.

WEDNESDAY, FEBRUARY 17
FIRST WEEK OF LENT

BEGIN

Spend a moment or two in silence. Set aside whatever might hinder your prayer.

PRAY

For you are not pleased with sacrifices; should I offer a burnt offering, you would not accept it. My sacrifice, O God, is a contrite spirit; a heart contrite and humbled, O God, you will not spurn.

~Psalm 51:18–19

LISTEN

Read Luke 11:29–32.

While still more people gathered in the crowd, Jesus said to them, "This generation is an evil generation; it seeks a sign, but no sign will be given it, except the sign of Jonah. Just as Jonah became a sign to the Ninevites, so will the Son of Man be to this generation."

~Luke 11:29–30

The Sign of Discipleship

I met Monsignor William N. Wall in the late 1950s when I was an altar server at my parish church in New Jersey. He got my attention because he wore khaki pants and sneakers under his cassock, the first priest I knew who wore anything but black clerical clothing. He was not to be trifled with; he frequently paused during Mass and glared at people who were disruptive and sometimes even bluntly rebuked them. More importantly, in a nearby city he founded and ran the Mount Carmel Guild, where he helped indigent men who were addicted to alcohol. He took these men in, cleaned them up, and put them to work. In my young life, Monsignor Wall provided the first example of ministry going outside the walls of the church and the boundaries of the parish and touching people regardless of their backgrounds.

Monsignor Wall was a no-nonsense guy. He didn't wait for signs to convince him of Jesus' authority; he simply took the Gospel to heart and got busy living it in the real world. He was an extraordinary man, and yet he was doing in his way what Jesus calls us all to do in our ways. Jesus said the only sign for the people of his generation would be the "sign of Jonah." That sign was the Resurrection. As we anticipate our celebration of Jesus' triumph over sin and death, we need no other sign to impel us to go into the world as his missionary disciples.

ACT

I will reflect on who or what has been a sign for me as to how I should live as a disciple of Christ. What has that sign inspired me to do?

PRAY

Lord Jesus, your sacrifice and resurrection are signs to me that life and good can triumph over death and sin. Help me to follow your example and that of your disciples through the ages so that I, too, may be an instrument through which you heal and comfort the world. Amen.

Thursday, February 18
First Week of Lent

BEGIN

Spend a moment or two in silence. Set aside whatever might hinder your prayer.

PRAY

When I called, you answered me; you built up strength within me.

~*Psalm 138:3*

LISTEN

Read Matthew 7:7–12.

"For everyone who asks, receives; and the one who seeks, finds; and to the one who knocks, the door will be opened."

~*Matthew 7:8*

Pray, Pray Always

Élisabeth Arrighi married Félix Leseur in France in 1889, but their bond was plagued by religious differences. Shortly before they married, Élisabeth learned that Félix had stopped practicing the Catholic faith. After their marriage, he became editor of a Paris newspaper that opposed organized religion—the Catholic Church in particular—and promoted atheism. He also ridiculed his wife's Catholicism and for a while shook her commitment. But eventually his aggressiveness caused her to delve more deeply into the faith, and she became profoundly spiritual. She wrote widely and performed such charitable works as her health would allow, but her primary focus became praying for the conversion of her husband.

Élisabeth died of cancer in 1914. After her death, Félix discovered her spiritual writing, which he had been unaware of before, including a letter to him concerning her prayers for his conversion. Still skeptical, he visited the shrine at Lourdes and at last experienced that conversion. In 1923, he was ordained a Dominican priest, and he served for twenty-seven years. He devoted a lot of his time and energy to publishing and speaking about Élisabeth's spiritual writing.

Persistence in prayer sustained Élisabeth; the example of her prayer evangelized Félix. Praying as Élisabeth did, and as Jesus urged us to, makes our personal encounter with God real and vital. When we express our faith in God by bringing our joys and sorrows to him—not demanding a certain response but submitting to his will—we find that he is not only the invisible Creator but also our most steadfast companion.

ACT

I will focus on the person who is most in need of prayer that I am aware of and try to pray for that person's needs for a few moments every day.

PRAY

O God, you know all of our needs before we bring them to you. Still, by our prayer we express our faith that you are always present and attentive to your people. Graciously hear us as we make our petitions, especially for those who have no one else to pray for them. Amen.

Friday, February 19
First Week of Lent

BEGIN

Spend a minute or two in silence. Set aside whatever might hinder your prayer.

PRAY

If you, O LORD, mark iniquities, LORD, who can stand? But with you is forgiveness, that you may be revered.

~Psalm 130:3–4

LISTEN

Read Matthew 5:20–26.

"You have heard that it was said to your ancestors, *You shall not kill; and whoever kills will be liable to judgment*. But I say to you, whoever is angry with his brother will be liable to judgment."

~Matthew 5:21–22a

"Forgive Them, Father . . ."

When adults whom I encounter in my ministry tell me that they find forgiveness to be the most challenging aspect of our faith, I always agree. Letting go of slights, betrayals, unfaithfulness, and violence is, indeed, challenging. But it is what we are called to, as we learn from Jesus in more than one passage of the gospels.

I sometimes use the example of Corrie ten Boom, a Christian woman who lived in the Netherlands during the Holocaust and who joined her father and other relatives to hide Jewish people from the Nazis. Eventually the whole ten Boom family was arrested,

and Corrie and her sister Betsie were sent to a concentration camp at Ravensbrück, Germany, where
Betsie died. In 1947, Corrie spoke in Munich on the
theme of forgiveness. After her talk, a man from the
audience approached her, and she recognized him as
a guard at the concentration camp. He thanked her for
her talk and remarked that it was good to know that
God forgives our sins. He acknowledged that he had
been a guard at Ravensbrück and explained that he
had become a Christian. He offered his hand to Corrie who, as she later wrote, was filled with revulsion.
But her own message to that audience welled up in
her, and she grasped the man's hand and told him she
forgave him.

Most of us will never have to forgive an offense of
that magnitude, and yet forgiveness even on that level
is what Jesus calls us to.

ACT

I will spend time in prayer about any anger or
resentment I may be entertaining against another
person. Remembering that Jesus forgave even those
who put him to death, I will try to replace my ran-
cor with a gesture of conciliation—a note, a card, or
a phone call.

PRAY

Dear Jesus, you gave us the most sublime example of forgiveness by praying for those who were
taking your life. Help me to imitate you by forgiving those who have wounded me, no matter how
serious the offense. May I always be a source of the
peace that you desire for the world. Amen.

Saturday, February 20
First Week of Lent

BEGIN

Spend a minute or two in silence. Set aside whatever might hinder your prayer.

PRAY

You have commanded that your precepts be diligently kept. Oh, that I might be firm in the ways of keeping your statutes!

~Psalm 119:4–5

LISTEN

Read Matthew 5:43–48.

"But I say to you, love your enemies, and pray for those who persecute you, that you may be children of your heavenly Father, for he makes his sun rise on the bad and the good, and causes rain to fall on the just and the unjust."

~Matthew 5:44–45

Fellow Travelers

When Durham, North Carolina, faced school integration in the 1970s, Ann Atwater was a leader in the black community, and C. P. Ellis was head of the local Ku Klux Klan. Feelings between them were so bitter that Ann once took out a knife to attack C. P. during a public gathering but was stopped by her friends.

When a court ordered Durham's schools to integrate, the two agreed to cochair community meetings to decide how to implement the order. Forced into each other's company, Ann and C. P. discovered their common interests, including their concern for the safety and education of their children and their impotence as poor people in a local society dominated by white and black middle classes. Because of their dialogue, C. P. realized that the black people he had despised were really fellow travelers on life's journey. He publicly destroyed his KKK card and became a leader of black and white unions in Durham. Ann and he became faithful friends.

It is simple to respond to this story by calling it extraordinary. But as Christians, we are called to do the extraordinary when "extraordinary" means recognizing the humanity we share with everyone on earth, even enemies of our nation and our way of life. We cannot come face-to-face with all of them or personally influence them the way Ann Atwater influenced C. P. Ellis; however, we can love them as brothers and sisters created in God's image and pray that God will inspire them to find fulfillment in ways that honor his law and human dignity.

ACT

I will ask the Holy Spirit to help me think of all people, including those I regard as enemies, first of all as brothers and sisters responding to the circumstances of their lives.

PRAY

Lord Jesus, you taught us with the story of the Good Samaritan that our "enemy" is also our neighbor. Help me to take that lesson to heart and to pray only that all people might act on the best impulses of the human nature our Creator gave us. Amen.

SUNDAY, FEBRUARY 21
SECOND WEEK OF LENT

BEGIN

Spend a minute or two in silence. Set aside whatever might hinder your prayer.

PRAY

Join with others in being imitators of me, brothers and sisters, and observe those who thus conduct themselves according to the model you have in us.

~*Philippians 3:17*

LISTEN

Read Luke 9:28b–36.

As they were about to part from him, Peter said to Jesus, "Master, it is good that we are here; let us make three tents, one for you, one for Moses, and one for Elijah." But he did not know what he was saying.

~*Luke 9:33*

We Are an Easter People

When I was a newspaper editor, my friend Dave Bixel told me about a Russian woman whose grandmother had come to New Jersey to visit, stayed after her visa expired, and now was lapsing into dementia. Because of the immigration issue, the young woman was reluctant to seek help. Dave wanted to know what I could do about it.

The women didn't live in my newspaper's market, and their legal problem seemed intractable, but Dave was unfazed by my pessimism. I called the appropriate congressman and—to my surprise—reached an attorney who said he would resolve the grandmother's immigration status.

I learned that lesson repeatedly from Dave: you can do more than you think you can. Dave specialized in fundraising for nonprofit organizations. In his professional and personal life, he thought big and therefore achieved big things for folks in need. His death in a highway accident at the age of fifty-six seemed to me to be the height of injustice.

In time, however, I came to see in Dave's life and death the message of the Transfiguration. The disciples who glimpsed the divinity of Jesus would soon have to cope with his unjust death and remain faithful to him and his Gospel in spite of that. Those who knew Dave gained nothing from that exhilarating experience unless we emerged, like the disciples, from our dismay over his death, remembering what we learned from him and living as he lived.

ACT

I will pray for someone I know who is experiencing difficulties and who would benefit from faith in God's grace. If possible, I will contact that person and make myself a sign of God's love.

PRAY

Lord Jesus, your disciples were thrilled at the signs of your divinity but recoiled from the prospect of your suffering and death. Help me to accept patiently the physical or emotional pain that may be part of my life, and help me to be confident in your companionship through these trials and in your promise of eternal life. Amen.

Monday, February 22
The Chair of St. Peter

BEGIN

Spend a minute or two in silence. Set aside whatever might hinder your prayer.

PRAY

Even though I walk in the dark valley I fear no evil; for you are at my side with your rod and your staff that give me courage.

~Psalm 23:4

LISTEN

Read Matthew 16:13–19.

"Who do people say that the Son of Man is?" They replied, "Some say John the Baptist, others Elijah, still others Jeremiah or one of the prophets." He said to them, "But who do you say that I am?" Simon Peter said in reply, "You are the Christ, the Son of the living God."

~Matthew 16:13b–16

Upon This Rock

Visiting the Basilica of St. Peter in Rome, especially for the first time, can be overwhelming. The sheer size of the structure—the largest church in the world—the vaulted ceilings, the soaring dome, and the multitude of altars and heroic monuments can be difficult to absorb. But there is a focal point both visibly and spiritually—the main altar designed by Gian Lorenzo Bernini and completed in 1653. The centerpiece of this altar is a gilt bronze sarcophagus in the shape of a chair; within is an actual wooden chair, dating from the ninth century and traditionally venerated as the chair used by Peter, the chief of the apostles and the first bishop of Rome.

The Church has set aside this day—even when it falls during Lent—in order to reflect on that chair, not as an important object in itself but as a symbol of the unity that Jesus wanted for his followers. That unity is grounded in our shared faith in Jesus as the Son of God and the savior of the world, in our mutual commitment to live in keeping with his Gospel of love, and our identification with each other as members of his body, the Church. Whenever we sin, either by an overt act or by neglect, we harm the Body of Christ and undermine the unity Jesus prayed for. By contrast, as we refresh our relationship with God during Lent, we contribute new vitality to the life of the whole Church.

ACT

Today, I will pray the Nicene Creed, reflecting after each phrase how my faith in the teachings of the Church unite me with Catholic men and women around the world and across time.

PRAY

Lord Jesus Christ, you prayed that your followers might be one as you and the Father are one. May I be an instrument of the unity you desire by remaining faithful to your Gospel and by witnessing to it through a life of service to others. Amen.

TUESDAY, FEBRUARY 23
SECOND WEEK OF LENT

BEGIN

Spend a minute or two in silence. Set aside whatever might hinder your prayer.

PRAY

Make justice your aim: redress the wronged, hear the orphan's plea, defend the widow.

~Isaiah 1:17b

LISTEN

Read Matthew 23:1–12.

"The greatest among you must be your servant. Whoever exalts himself will be humbled; but whoever humbles himself will be exalted."

~Matthew 23:11–12

The First Shall Be Last

There's a story often told about George Washington that actually involved one of his generals. Jacob Francis, a black soldier who enlisted in a Massachusetts regiment during the American Revolution, reported the incident.

According to Francis, he and his fellow soldiers were building a fortification during the defense of Boston when Major General Israel Putnam rode up to observe the work. As Putnam watched, he addressed one soldier as "my lad" and told him to pick up a stone and throw it onto the middle of the fortification. The young man put his hand to his hat and told Putnam, "Sir, I am a corporal." "I ask your pardon, sir," Putnam said; he then dismounted, threw the stone onto the breastwork himself, got back on his horse, and rode off.

The lesson in humility that Putnam gave the corporal was consistent with what Jesus taught in the remarks recorded in Matthew's gospel. Jesus didn't question the need for levels of authority in human affairs, but he did caution his followers against thinking that positions of authority made them intrinsically superior to those whom they directed. On the contrary, Jesus taught that the needs of others and the general welfare should take precedence over the pride of overseers—whatever form their authority might take. Whatever titles we may have—parent, teacher, supervisor, pastor, police officer—our vocation as Christians is still to serve our brothers and sisters.

ACT

I will prayerfully reflect on situations in my life in which I may be in a position of authority—as an employer, a supervisor, a teacher, a grandparent or parent, or a customer dealing with people who work in service such as waiters and waitresses, busboys, porters, and checkout clerks. I will pray for the grace to be considerate of others in all such relationships.

PRAY

Lord Jesus, although you were God, scripture tells us that you "emptied" yourself, taking on "the form of a slave" in order to carry out the earthly ministry that has made it possible for us to share in your divinity. Help me to remember that no matter what I achieve or what I acquire in life, my true vocation is to imitate you by serving my brothers and sisters. Amen.

WEDNESDAY, FEBRUARY 24
SECOND WEEK OF LENT

BEGIN

Spend a minute or two in silence. Set aside whatever might hinder your prayer.

PRAY

Into your hands I commend my spirit; you will redeem me, O LORD, O faithful God.

~Psalm 31:6

LISTEN

Read Matthew 20:17–28.

"Whoever wishes to be great among you shall be your servant; whoever wishes to be first among you shall be your slave. Just so, the Son of Man did not come to be served but to serve and to give his life as a ransom for many."

~Matthew 20:26b–28

To Serve, Not to Be Served

Richard Parks was a professional Welsh rugby player for thirteen years until a shoulder injury forced him to retire in 2009. After his retirement, he announced that he would attempt to climb the highest mountain on each of the seven continents and stand on the North Pole, the South Pole, and the summit of Mount Everest—all within seven months. He achieved his ambition, and because his grandmother, father, and uncle had suffered from cancer, he used the self-challenge to raise the equivalent of hundreds of thousands of dollars for Marie Curie Cancer Care.

Richard Parks had this in common with the apostles James and John, the sons of Zebedee, or at least with their mother: they were ambitious. In itself, ambition is neither good nor bad. Its moral quality depends on how it is directed. Parks, no doubt frustrated by the premature end of his career, used his ambition to show that he was still capable of mighty feats. But he also applied his energy to supporting and providing publicity to an important charity. By contrast, the ambition of James and John (who, Mark's gospel says, personally asked Jesus for the places of honor) seemed directed only at their aggrandizement.

In spite of the rebuke by Jesus, the brothers continued to follow him and, after his resurrection and ascension, literally went out to teach all nations as Jesus had commanded them. The incident we read about today was a part of their formation; they learned from it. May we apply the same lesson to ourselves by being ambitious not for power, prestige, or material gain but for the well-being of others.

ACT

I will take stock of my goals and ambitions: where I want to go, what I want to become, how I want to spend my time, and what I want to acquire. Then I will commit myself to sacrificing one of these goals so that I might serve the needs of others.

PRAY

Lord Jesus Christ, you were the Son of God and yet you set aside the glory due to you and experienced rejection, persecution, and death so that we might gain eternal life. Help us to imitate you by preferring the common good to our personal status and comfort. Amen.

Thursday, February 25
Second Week of Lent

BEGIN

Spend a minute or two in silence. Set aside whatever might hinder your prayer.

PRAY

For the LORD watches over the way of the just, but the way of the wicked vanishes.

~Psalm 1:6

LISTEN

Read Luke 16:19–31.

Jesus said to the Pharisees: "There was a rich man who dressed in purple garments and fine linen and dined sumptuously each day. And lying at his door was a poor man named Lazarus, covered with sores, who would gladly have eaten his fill of the scraps that fell from the rich man's table."

~Luke 16:19–21a

Travel Far and Wide

We usually associate Charles Dickens with Advent, not with Lent, but the central theme of his novella *A Christmas Carol* reflects the point Jesus made with the story of the rich man and Lazarus. In the parable, we hear the rich man futilely trying in death to intercede for the well-being of his living brothers after spending a lifetime thinking of no one but himself. In Dickens's story, we hear the ghost of Jacob Marley warning Ebenezer Scrooge of the fate that awaits selfish people: "It is required of every man," Marley tells his former business partner, "that the spirit within him should walk abroad among his fellow-men, and travel far and wide; and if that spirit goes not forth in life, it is condemned to do so after death. It is doomed to wander through the world—oh, woe is me!—and witness what it cannot share, but might have shared on earth, and turned to happiness!" Before departing, the ghost lets Scrooge momentarily glimpse the shadows of the condemned: "The misery with them all was, clearly, that they sought to interfere, for good, in human matters, and had lost the power for ever."

Pope Francis often urges us to seek out the poor and minister to them. The irony in the parable is that the rich man didn't have to "travel far and wide" to find an opportunity to relieve human misery; the opportunity lay on his doorstep. Neither would any of us have to search very far to find want, pain, or loneliness that we have the power to relieve.

ACT

I will seek and take advantage of an opportunity— such as volunteering at a soup kitchen, food pantry, or nursing home—to directly help the poor.

PRAY

Father in Heaven, help me to see the many ways in which I am capable of helping the poor, and give me the will to use my gifts—time, talent, and material resources—to ease the want and suffering of my brothers and sisters. Amen.

FRIDAY, FEBRUARY 26
SECOND WEEK OF LENT

BEGIN

Spend a minute or two in silence. Set aside whatever might hinder your prayer.

PRAY

Remember the marvels the Lord has done.

~*Psalm 105:5a*

LISTEN

Read Matthew 21:33–43, 45–46.

Jesus said to them, "Did you never read in the Scriptures: The stone that the builders rejected has become the cornerstone; by the Lord has this been done, and it is wonderful in our eyes?"

~*Matthew 21:42*

A Friend Like Jesus

My high school class has had several reunions since our graduation in 1960. Although many of our classmates have attended and others have at least kept in touch with us, there are several whom we have not heard from in more than fifty years. No doubt this is true in part because some people are not nostalgic and are not charmed by reliving their past. Some may be ill or troubled in another way. But there were also some boys and girls who were not treated well in high school and who might not wish to be reminded of it. These were the handful of our peers who didn't fit in and were therefore abused, ridiculed, shunned, or simply ignored. We remember who they were, and we wonder to what extent we, even by simply doing nothing, contributed to their loneliness and pain.

Rejection was a factor in the life of Jesus too. The prophet Isaiah foretold it, speaking about the Messiah who would be "despised and rejected by others" (53:3), and we read in the Gospel of John that "his own people did not accept him" (1:11, NRSV). But Jesus did not reject others. In fact, he confounded the mores of his time by opening his heart to those who were routinely rejected by their community: the disabled, the destitute, lepers, tax collectors, prostitutes, Samaritans, and Gentiles. If we are his disciples, we will imitate his example by offering our presence, our attention, our kindness, and our assistance to those who would otherwise be left out.

ACT

I will make a conscious effort to notice anyone in my parish or in my community whom others ignore or even avoid. On my own or with my neighbors or fellow parishioners, I will try to bring some warmth and friendship to that person's life.

PRAY

Lord Jesus, you called on us to imitate you by unconditionally loving our neighbors and especially those whom no one seems to love. Give me the prudence, judgment, and greatness of heart to be a source of comfort to those who are most alone in the world. Amen.

BEGIN

Spend a minute or two in silence. Set aside whatever might hinder your prayer.

PRAY

For as the heavens are high above the earth, so surpassing is his kindness toward those who fear him. As far as the east is from the west, so far has he put our transgressions from us.

~Psalm 103:11–12

LISTEN

Read Luke 15:1–3, 11–32.

"Now we must celebrate and rejoice, because your brother was dead and has come to life again; he was lost and has been found."

~Luke 15:32

Begin Again

Roy Riegels was just twenty years old, but he felt as if his life was over. Riegels played center for the University of California, Berkeley, in the 1929 Rose Bowl Game against Georgia Tech. In the second quarter, Riegels retrieved a Tech fumble about thirty yards from Tech's end zone, but in the confusion he ran sixty-nine yards in the wrong direction until he was stopped at Tech's one-yard line. At halftime, Riegels sat alone and wept, but coach Nibs Price announced that the same team that started the game would start the second half. "I can't do it," Riegels told him. "I've ruined you. I've ruined myself. . . . I couldn't face that crowd to save my life." But Price told him to get out on the field. Riegels did play, and he played well, although Tech eventually won the game. He was team captain and an All-American the following season. In later life, he taught, coached scholastic football, served in the Army Air Corps, and was a respected businessman.

Nibs Price had watched Riegels commit perhaps the biggest blunder in collegiate football, but even with the Rose Bowl Game and his own reputation on the line, he gave the young man a second chance. The parable of the father and his sons is about second chances. Jesus is about second chances. God, who prefers mercy to punishment, is about second chances—or as many chances as it takes. And Lent is an opportunity for us to turn to God, acknowledge the ways in which we haven't fully lived the Gospel, and with his blessing, begin again.

ACT

I will receive the Sacrament of Reconciliation and resolve to extend to others the patience and mercy God has shown to me.

PRAY

Merciful God, when I open my heart to you like the young man of the parable returning to his father, accept my penance and my determination to renew my life and to joyfully share my peace with the world. Amen.

SUNDAY, FEBRUARY 28
THIRD WEEK OF LENT

BEGIN

Spend a minute or two in silence. Set aside whatever might hinder your prayer.

PRAY

He redeems your life from destruction, he crowns you with kindness and compassion.

~Psalm 103:4

LISTEN

Read Luke 13:1–9.

"I tell you, if you do not repent, you will all perish as they did!"

~Luke 13:5

Repent and Live

One of the passions in my father's life was baseball—New York Yankees baseball. When the Yankees were at home, Dad and a friend haunted the stadium, and when my brother and I showed interest, he took us too. During home stands, we sat in the same box a dozen or so rows behind the Yankee dugout about three times a week. Because we were regulars, we became familiar with the ushers and with other fanatical ticket-holders. Among the latter was an elderly couple who sat near us; they always dressed as if they were going to church—which, in the 1950s and 1960s, meant that they dressed well. One April, after we had gone to a few games, we missed that couple. My dad mentioned it to one of the ushers who told us that they had been murdered during a robbery at a clothing store they owned in Manhattan.

That incident marked the first time that something such as murder came uncomfortably close to my young life. The report that those folks had been shot to death immediately prompted in me the question raised by the massacre of the Galileans and the eighteen deaths in the catastrophe at Siloam: why should such a thing happen to innocent people? Those who asked Jesus about that were implying what was commonly held at that time—that such disasters were God's punishment on sinful people. But Jesus rejected the idea that the victims were more sinful than anyone else in Galilee or Jerusalem and advised his audience to stop justifying punishment of others and instead turn around their own lives so as to avoid a worse fate—the loss of eternal life.

ACT

I will consciously release any judgments I have made about others, and I will ask God to forgive me for harboring those thoughts and give me the grace to avoid them in the future.

PRAY

Merciful God, help me to consider all people as my brothers and sisters, bound on the same journey and subject to the same challenges, and give me the wisdom to leave judgment to you. Amen.

MONDAY, FEBRUARY 29
THIRD WEEK OF LENT

BEGIN

Spend a minute or two in silence. Set aside whatever might hinder your prayer.

PRAY

Athirst is my soul for God, the living God. When shall I go and behold the face of God?

~*Psalm 42:3*

LISTEN

Read Luke 4:24–30.

Jesus said to the people in the synagogue at Nazareth. . . . "Again, there were many lepers in Israel during the time of Elisha the prophet; yet not one of them was cleansed, but only Naaman the Syrian." When the people in the synagogue heard this, they were all filled with fury.

~*Luke 4:24, 27–28*

Love One Another

When I was editor of a daily newspaper, we periodically invited about a dozen readers to discuss the newspaper and the community. At one such gathering, I distributed copies of a weekly Spanish-language newspaper that we also published. One woman angrily asked why we, as she put it, encouraged people to use Spanish instead of learning English—a complaint that often masks a deeper resentment of immigrants. I explained that the weekly served the needs of recent immigrants who had not yet mastered English and that many others who read the weekly also read our

English daily. She was not sympathetic. Later, when the subject had changed, the same woman said with a laugh, "My mother came here from Greece sixty years ago, and she still doesn't speak a word of English!"

The Old and New Testaments confirm that antagonism toward people from other cultures is nothing new. When Jesus told his neighbors in small, insular Nazareth that foreigners might be more likely than they to accept his teaching, their reaction was violent but not unfamiliar. In our own time, global communications can promote understanding among people of different beliefs and backgrounds; unfortunately, this technology has also demonstrated its power to broadcast stereotypes and fan paranoia and hatred. We disciples of Jesus are called to be more thoughtful, to see in faces of every description the face of God. As Pope Francis has reminded us, we are called to "listen to one another, to make plans together, and in this way to overcome suspicion and prejudice, and to build a coexistence that is ever more secure, peaceful, and inclusive."

ACT

I will make a point of being open-minded and welcoming whenever and wherever I meet people whose ethnic or religious backgrounds are different from my own.

PRAY

Creator God, our world, which exists only because of your will, is adorned with diversity. Give me the freedom of spirit to rejoice in the diversity among my fellow human beings and to treat people of every description with dignity and appreciation. Amen.

Tuesday, March 1
Third Week of Lent

BEGIN

Spend a minute or two in silence. Set aside whatever might hinder your prayer.

PRAY

He guides the humble to justice, he teaches the humble his way.

~Psalm 25:9

LISTEN

Read Matthew 18:21–35.

His master summoned him and said to him, "You wicked servant! I forgave you your entire debt because you begged me to. Should you not have had pity on your fellow servant, as I had pity on you?"

~Matthew 18:32–33

"I Firmly Resolve . . . to Sin No More"

In April 1830, George Wilson and James Porter were handed six indictments for robbing the mail and assaulting a mail driver in Pennsylvania. Though they pleaded not guilty on all accounts, the jury found both men guilty and, for endangering the life of the mail carrier, sentenced them to death. The following day Porter was executed, and later that month Wilson changed his plea to guilty. In June of that year, President Andrew Jackson pardoned Wilson with respect to the death penalty, but Wilson—without explaining himself—declined the pardon. Through a complicated legal process, the US Supreme Court in 1833 considered the odd question of whether Wilson, or any convicted person, can reject a pardon. Chief Justice John Marshall, describing a pardon as "an act of grace," wrote, "It may . . . be rejected by the person to whom it is tendered, . . . we have discovered no power in a court to force it on him."

The parable of the unforgiving servant is another story of pardon granted and rejected. No doubt the servant was glad that the king had forgiven a large debt. Who wouldn't be? But the king's mercy did not touch the servant's heart; it did not inspire an interior conversion in him. Although the king later withdrew his pardon, it was really the mean-spirited servant who rejected it by proving himself unworthy.

God has promised to forgive our sins if we repent, but repentance doesn't mean only a sigh of relief. The word implies a turning away from sin toward a better life—in other words, a conversion. Accepting God's pardon means resolving to change our lives.

ACT

I will examine my conscience and make a sincere act of contrition; I will rejoice in the ways my renewed spirit affects the routine business of my life today.

PRAY

O God in Heaven, you are mercy itself. I acknowledge to you my failings, and I pledge to you that the grace of your forgiveness will radiate from me to warm the lives of everyone I meet. Amen.

Wednesday, March 2
Third Week of Lent

BEGIN

Spend a minute or two in silence. Set aside whatever might hinder your prayer.

PRAY

He sends forth his command to the earth; swiftly runs his word!

~*Psalm 147:15*

LISTEN

Read Matthew 5:17–19.

"Amen, I say to you, until heaven and earth pass away, not the smallest letter or the smallest part of a letter will pass from the law."

~*Matthew 5:18*

Written in Our Hearts

On December 1, 1955, Rosa Parks boarded a bus in Montgomery, Alabama, and sat in the eleventh row of seats. Under a Montgomery ordinance, the first ten rows on a city bus were reserved for white people. But the bus was crowded, and the driver told Mrs. Parks that she would have to move to make room for white passengers. Mrs. Parks refused, arguing that she was acting within the law, but the driver argued that the law empowered him to separate white and black passengers. The driver called the police, Mrs. Parks was arrested, and the incident sparked the historic Montgomery bus boycott. While Mrs. Parks's conviction was being appealed, a US District Court and then the US

Supreme Court ruled that the Montgomery city law was no law at all—it was unconstitutional.

Rosa Parks dramatized the principle that law does not exist so stronger people can oppress weaker people. That's why the Montgomery law was no law at all. When Jesus said the smallest detail of the law would remain in place, he was not referring to the myriad of dietary and purity regulations that had been imposed on the Jewish people over several generations. He was referring to the law imparted through Moses and summarized in the Ten Commandments: the law that teaches us to indiscriminately love one another as God has loved us. Jesus criticized pointless regulations that weighed people down and did nothing to help them, but he upheld the law that is written in our hearts, the law we obey not out of fear but out of love.

ACT

I will be conscious of how I live the Gospel in my observance of such things as speed limits and environmental regulations that are designed to protect the common good.

PRAY

Loving God, your law teaches us to care for each other and for the world in which we live. Help me to apply that law to every decision I make and every action I take in my daily life. Amen.

Thursday, March 3
Third Week of Lent

BEGIN

Spend a minute or two in silence. Set aside whatever might hinder your prayer.

PRAY

Come, let us bow down in worship; let us kneel before the LORD who made us. For he is our God, and we are the people he shepherds, the flock he guides.

~Psalm 95:6–7

LISTEN

Read Luke 11:14–23.

"If it is by the finger of God that I drive out demons, then the Kingdom of God has come upon you."

~Luke 11:20

Keeping Good Company

In 1954, William Golding published a novel about a group of boys marooned on a remote Pacific island. In this story, Golding related how the boys' little society deteriorated into chaos as their worst instincts over-whelmed any sense of a common good. The inner demon stifling the boys' better nature provided the novel's title and is known as "the lord of the flies." "The lord of the flies," in turn, is a translation of "Beel-zebul," the name used by Jesus and his critics to refer to the devil.

Some of the folks who saw Jesus rid the speechless man of a demon could not rejoice in the fact that their neighbor had been made whole; instead, they let their own inner demons take over as they challenged Jesus, insisting that his power to heal must come from an evil source. This impulse to be cynical and self-centered and to disregard the well-being of our neighbor can arise at any time in everyday life. We may not recognize Beelzebul, but he's lurking nearby when we engage in destructive gossip; when we speed or cut off other drivers so we can be first by a few seconds; when we are rude to service people such as waiters, cashiers, or gas station attendants; or when we use hurtful language to contradict or belittle family members, coworkers, or friends. This impulse can be checked by a life of prayer in which we are in constant conversation with our Savior. When we invite the companionship of Jesus, we keep the lord of the flies at bay.

ACT

I will take the time to review my day and ask myself when I thought of my own benefit instead of the welfare of others. If there were such times, I will pray for forgiveness. If there were no such times, I will thank God for his grace.

PRAY

Loving God, I know that you are present everywhere and at all times. I pray that everything I think, say, and do each day will be blessed by my awareness of your presence. Be close to me always in the person of your Son, Jesus Christ. Amen.

Friday, March 4
Third Week of Lent

BEGIN

Spend a minute or two in silence. Set aside whatever might hinder your prayer.

PRAY

"There shall be no strange god among you nor shall you worship any alien god."

~*Psalm 81:10*

LISTEN

Read Mark 12:28–34.

One of the scribes came to Jesus and asked him, "Which is the first of all the commandments?" Jesus replied, "The first is this: *Hear, O Israel! The Lord our God is Lord alone! You shall love the Lord your God with all your heart, with all your soul, with all your mind, and with all your strength.*"

~*Mark 12:28–30*

"The Lord Is One"

I once read a blog post in which a priest told of a frivolous contest run by a radio station. Listeners to the station were invited to set their clock radios to that station and, when they got up in the morning, call and report the first words they had said that day. The third caller each day would win $106, the same number as the station's radio frequency. Responses included "Do I smell coffee burning?" and "Honey, did I put the dog out last night?" But one morning the third caller said something unexpected. His first words had been, "Hear, O Israel, the LORD our God, the LORD is one."

That man had begun the day by saying the prayer known in Hebrew as *Shema Yisrael*, which is taken from Deuteronomy 6:4–9. This declaration of the oneness of God is so important in Jewish tradition that when Jesus was asked what was first among the commandments, he referred not to the Decalogue but to the *Shema*. Observant Jews recite this prayer the first thing in the morning and the last thing at night, they teach it to their children, and they hope it will be last words they say before dying. It is part of a tradition in which prayer is a central component of everyday life.

The man who called the radio station provided a good example to all believers. Beginning the day by acknowledging God is a good start to keeping God at the forefront of our thoughts during the activities of our daily lives. Even the simplest prayer in the morning can lead to a whole day dedicated to the one God and to none of the other "gods" that can preoccupy us.

ACT

I will begin during this season to develop the habit of acknowledging God with praise and gratitude at the beginning of each day of my life.

PRAY

All-powerful God, I thank you for the gift of each day of my life. Give me the grace to make each day, even in its simplest details, a sign of my love for you and my gratitude for your love. Amen.

Saturday, March 5
Third Week of Lent

BEGIN

Spend a minute or two in silence. Set aside whatever might hinder your prayer.

PRAY

Have mercy on me, O God, in your goodness; in the greatness of your compassion wipe out my offense.

~Psalm 51:3

LISTEN

Read Luke 18:9–14.

"But the tax collector stood off at a distance and would not even raise his eyes to heaven but beat his breast and prayed, 'O God, be merciful to me a sinner.'"

~Luke 18:13

Submit to God's Mercy

The parable of the tax collector and the Pharisee calls to mind a story that is usually attributed to Frederick II, also called "the Great," king of Prussia for more than forty years in the eighteenth century. The story goes that Frederick visited a prison and spoke with several of the inmates. One after another, the inmates told the king that they were imprisoned unjustly. Frederick approached one man by saying, "And you. I suppose you're innocent, too?" "No, majesty," the man said. "I'm guilty, and I deserve to be punished." Frederick then turned to the jailer and said, "Release this man. I don't want him corrupting all these innocent victims!"

Our Christian faith is not about guilt but about mercy. But in order to be in a right relationship with God, we must acknowledge our mistakes as did that last prisoner, sincerely commit ourselves to avoid them in the future, and ask for the forgiveness that God has promised us. When we have repented and received God's grace, our previous failings need no longer weigh us down. The Pharisee is convinced of the human failings of the tax collector but cannot admit to the weaknesses he himself certainly has. He stands in the way of his own salvation. The tax collector, on the other hand, knows who he is and knows that he must—and can—be reconciled with God. When he has done that, his sins will be as nothing. At the moment described in Jesus' story, the tax collector experiences a "little Lent," and he gives us a model to imitate during this holy season.

ACT

I will consider adopting the "Examen of Consciousness" of St. Ignatius Loyola as a daily exercise (see "The Daily Examen," Ignatian Spirituality, ignatianspirituality.com). I will review my daily life for the past week and make an act of contrition.

PRAY

O God, the prophets and the psalms spoke of your mercy. Jesus, your Son, proclaimed it in his teaching and practiced it in his ministry. I submit to you all of my human failings, confident that you extend your mercy to me, accept my penitence, and embrace me as your loved one. Amen.

Sunday, March 6
Fourth Week of Lent

BEGIN

Spend a minute or two in silence. Set aside whatever might hinder your prayer.

PRAY

I sought the LORD, and he answered me and delivered me from all my fears.

~Psalm 34:5

LISTEN

Read Luke 15:1–3, 11–32.

"But now we must celebrate and rejoice, because your brother was dead and has come to life again."

~Luke 15:32

A Time to Rejoice

The story Jesus told about the father and his sons may not have the same impact on us as it had on the folks who first heard it. In fact, our reaction to this story may be too casual: the father forgave his errant son; wasn't that nice?

But scholars tell us that Jesus meant for this story to be shocking. Jaime Cardinal Sin, who was then archbishop of Manila, pointed this out in an address he gave in 1999. The father in the tale is a metaphor for God, and Cardinal Sin said that the father running to greet his son is one of the most shocking images of God in the Bible. It was shocking because, in first-century Palestine, a father was an authority figure who would not belittle himself by rushing to a reprobate son even before hearing the boy's apologies. At best, a father would have waited at home for the boy to come to him. That kind of father squared with the kind of God most people believed in—a God who was remote, stern, and judgmental.

Jesus told that story in order to communicate the idea that the first and constant factor in our relationship with God is that God loves us. When we approach God in penance, as we do during this Lenten season, we do so with the assurance that he is already disposed to dismiss even the worst of our errors. Far from being a depressing season in which we wallow in guilt, Lent can be for us like the feast the father ordered for his prodigal son, a feast in which God rejoices in our homecoming and we rejoice in his mercy.

ACT

I will meditate on the aspects of my life that I would like to improve, make an act of contrition, and celebrate by doing something that makes me especially happy.

PRAY

O loving God, I place before you all the ways in which I have offended you by actions or by my neglect, and I celebrate with you that, through your grace, we are reconciled as parent and child. Amen.

MONDAY, MARCH 7
FOURTH WEEK OF LENT

BEGIN

Spend a minute or two in silence. Set aside whatever might hinder your prayer.

PRAY

Sing praise to the LORD, you his faithful ones, and give thanks to his holy name. For his anger lasts but a moment; a lifetime, his good will.

~Psalm 30:5–6a

LISTEN

Read John 4:43–54.

They told him, "The fever left him yesterday, about one in the afternoon." The father realized that just at that time Jesus had said to him, "Your son will live," and he and his whole household came to believe.

~John 4:52b–53

Trust in the Lord

In the 1977 movie *Oh, God!*, the Almighty recruits Jerry Landers to become a prophet to the modern world. The movie, a $51 million hit, was light on substance and heavy on platitudes. Many religious groups criticized it as sacrilegious. In a broad way, the movie evoked the experience of Moses who balked when God proposed to speak through him. Moses objected that he was not eloquent enough to confront Pharaoh and demand the liberation of the Hebrews. And Jerry Landers argued— correctly, as it turned out—that people wouldn't listen to him. At one point, "God" responded to this doubt by saying, "Trust me—like it says on the money."

Regardless of the shortcomings of the movie, that one line was good advice. We see the idea presented more sublimely in the account of the royal official who asked Jesus to help a son who was near death. There are conflicting opinions as to whether Jesus was addressing this official or curious bystanders with the remark, "Unless you people see signs and wonders, you will not believe." But when Jesus told the official, "You may go; your son will live," the official trusted him and set off for home. This is an important example for us during Lent—not because we may be asking God to heal us physically but because we are asking him to heal us spiritually. It's easy to become discouraged by our mistakes, but God has promised us that if we sincerely repent he will forgive us anything. We can approach our Lenten practices not with trepidation but with confidence because, after all, in God we trust.

ACT

I will focus my attention on the habit or mistake that plagues me most often. I will pray for the fortitude to avoid this problem in the future, thank God for forgiving my sins in the past, and dismiss any doubt that God will be with me as I continue my spiritual journey.

PRAY

O forgiving God, you know better than I do the missteps in my life. I am truly sorry for all of these. I am determined to live in keeping with the Gospel, and I trust in your promise to love me as I am, lift me up when I fall, and embrace me at the end of my life's journey. Amen.

TUESDAY, MARCH 8
FOURTH WEEK OF LENT

BEGIN

Spend a minute or two in silence. Set aside whatever might hinder your prayer.

PRAY

God is our refuge and our strength, an ever-present help in distress.

~*Psalm 46:2*

LISTEN

Read John 5:1–16.

"Look, you are well; do not sin any more, so that nothing worse may happen to you."

~*John 5:14b*

The Blame Game

Joe approached me before the third meeting of a college class I was teaching and asked if I would let him in. He had failed the course once, he said, although the instructor had admired his work. I let him join; he didn't complete one assignment. But that was the fault of the friend who borrowed Joe's laptop, the stranger who took Joe's briefcase, and the pal who needed a ride out of state—anyone but Joe.

Joe comes to mind in light of the cure of the paralyzed man. Although a disabled man is a sympathetic figure, this one was reluctant to take responsibility for himself. When Jesus asked if he wanted to be healed, the man didn't shout yes; instead, he made excuses for why he hadn't been healed before. People wouldn't help him; it was their fault. When folks asked the man why he was carrying his mat on the Sabbath, he didn't say he had just been cured of paralysis and was happy just to be able to stand. Instead, he said that "the man"—he hadn't thought to ask Jesus' name—had told him to carry it. It was "the man's" fault. And in their second encounter, Jesus implied he knew that many of the cured fellow's problems were of his own making.

People like Joe and the paralytic man aren't unusual in putting the blame on others. But Lent is an opportunity to be honest, with God and with ourselves, and to acknowledge the failings for which we are responsible—not so we can feel the embarrassment we've been trying to avoid but so we can start life anew knowing that God forgives us.

ACT

I will think about my life and single out one way in which I could be a better person—healthier, more productive, more patient, and more generous—and in which, through my own fault, I have not grown. Perhaps it is the problem I identified during yesterday's reflection; perhaps it is something else. I will resolve to act upon this one aspect of my life, and I will pray to God for the grace to persevere.

PRAY

Merciful God, like Eve who blamed the serpent for her sin and like Adam who blamed Eve, I may try at times to avoid responsibility for my actions. But you know me better than I know myself, and I pray for the courage to acknowledge my mistakes so that I can avoid them in the future and grow ever closer to you. Amen.

Wednesday, March 9
Fourth Week of Lent

BEGIN

Spend a minute or two in silence. Set aside whatever might hinder your prayer.

PRAY

The Lord is gracious and merciful, slow to anger and of great kindness. The Lord is good to all and compassionate toward all his works.

~Psalm 145:8–9

LISTEN

Read John 5:17–30.

"Whoever does not honor the Son does not honor the Father who sent him. Amen, amen, I say to you, whoever hears my word and believes in the one who sent me has eternal life and will not come to condemnation, but has passed from death to life."

~John 5:23b–24

"This Is My Beloved Son"

The author Salman Rushdie once described Dan Brown's *The Da Vinci Code* as "a novel so bad that it gives bad novels a bad name." Not all critics agreed with this assessment when the book was published in 2003, and good or bad, Brown's tale was a worldwide bestseller. But the Church and many Christians found the book offensive with its premise that Jesus had married Mary Magdalene and fathered children with her and with its suggestion that the doctrine that Jesus was both human and divine was fabricated in order to make Christianity more palatable to pagans who were accustomed to worshiping demigods.

Dan Brown was not the first, nor will he be the last, to challenge the central tenet of our faith: that Jesus has both the nature of humanity and the nature of God and that in his divine nature he is one in the Trinity with the Father and the Holy Spirit. But we Christians reflect on the teachings of Jesus not only because they show us the only path to peace and justice on earth but also because Jesus spoke with the authority of God. As we re-form our lives to bring them even more in tune with the values of the Gospel during Lent, we should not approach it as a self-help exercise. We should approach it as an encounter with the person, Jesus, who is the tangible sign of God's presence in the world and of God's inexhaustible love for us.

ACT

I will prayerfully read some stories of the compassion of Jesus, remembering that this compassion, which is the will of God, envelops me even in my imperfection. (See, for example, Luke 7:11–17, Luke 7:36–50, and John 8:3–11.)

PRAY

Loving God, in the person of Jesus you made possible for us an intimate relationship with you in the visible, tangible world. Help us to imitate Jesus by conforming our will to your will and to recognize in his love and mercy the grace that comes from your own infinite generosity. Amen.

THURSDAY, MARCH 10
FOURTH WEEK OF LENT

BEGIN

Spend a minute or two in silence. Set aside whatever might hinder your prayer.

PRAY

They forgot the God who had saved them, who had done great deeds in Egypt.

~*Psalm 106:21*

LISTEN

Read John 5:31–47.

"I came in the name of my Father, but you do not accept me; yet if another comes in his own name, you will accept him."

~*John 5:43*

Hear and Live the Gospel

An acquaintance of mine is absorbed by the divine forces in nature, spiritual healing, and figures such as the Dalai Lama. She posted on a social media site this statement by the Buddhist sage: "It is far more useful to be aware of a single shortcoming in ourselves than it is to be aware of a thousand in somebody else." I answered with a statement by Jesus: "How can you say to your brother, 'Brother, let me take out the speck that is in your eye' when you yourself cannot see the log that is in your own eye?" (Lk 6:42, RSV).

The Dalai Lama is often one of the most reasonable voices we hear. When he spoke at a university in New Jersey, there were far more people trying to get tickets than there were seats to accommodate them. Most of those people must have been at least nominally Christian. I wondered when they had been as eager to hear the teaching of Jesus. Jesus, the Son of God, set the standard for a moral life; no other authority is necessary. If his teaching hasn't transformed the world, it isn't because another teacher is needed; it's because the world hasn't taken the Gospel to heart and put it into practice in everyday life. In the new beginning that Lent represents, we can commit ourselves to read the Gospel regularly, listen attentively as it is preached, profess it without shame when it is challenged or neglected, and proclaim it ourselves by how we live every moment of every day.

ACT

I will prayerfully read the gospel passage to be proclaimed at next Sunday's Mass and then I will listen attentively to the reading and the homily, all the while considering how the scripture applies to my everyday life. I will talk to at least one other person about what insight I gained. I will sincerely try to make this a weekly practice. (Readings for daily Mass, including Sundays, can be found at the United States Conference of Catholic Bishops website: usccb.org.)

PRAY

Lord Jesus Christ, you told Pontius Pilate that you came into the world to bear witness to the truth. Help me to always listen first to your teaching and to live according to your word, for you are truth itself. Amen.

FRIDAY, MARCH 11
FOURTH WEEK OF LENT

Spend a minute or two in silence. Set aside whatever might hinder your prayer.

PRAY

Many are the troubles of the just man, but out of them all the LORD delivers him.

~Psalm 34:20

LISTEN

Read John 7:1–2, 10, 25–30.

So they tried to arrest him, but no one laid a hand upon him, because his hour had not yet come.

~John 7:30

The Other Cheek

In the 1985 film *Witness*, an Amish family—as part of a chain of events following a murder in Philadelphia—shelters policeman John Book. While he is with the family, Book and three young Amish men are harassed by a group of toughs. The nonviolent Amish take the harassment without responding, but John Book answers with his fists.

This scene raises a question: are we to admire the Amish men who were humiliated or the cop who triumphed over the bullies? When we're watching movies—so many of which involve violence responding to violence—the answer may seem clear, and, in fact, applause broke out in many theaters when that scene was shown.

But that is not the example Jesus gave us. In the gospel reading, we hear the rumblings of what will soon confront him: "Is he not the one they are trying to kill?" And we know that he will respond to betrayal, false accusations, verbal and physical abuse, and crucifixion with patience, not with retaliation.

And what of us, who are unlikely to be in a spot like John Book's? When someone makes a caustic remark, do we feel compelled to answer with something a little sharper? When someone cuts us off on the road, do we feel compelled to speed up and get in front again? Do we applaud as the good guy annihilates the bad guys in so many of the films and digital games of our time? Or do we take the counsel of the apostle Peter: "Do not return evil for evil or reviling for reviling; but on the contrary bless, for to this you have been called" (1 Pt 3:9, RSV)?

ACT

I will resolve today not to patronize movies, television shows, electronic games, or any other media that present violence as admirable or heroic. I will pray for an end to violence in the world.

PRAY

Gentle Jesus, you taught us not to answer insult with insult or violence with violence, and you gave us a challenging example by not striking back at your enemies. May I apply your teaching and imitate your example in every aspect of my life. Amen.

Saturday, March 12
Fourth Week of Lent

BEGIN

Spend a minute or two in silence. Set aside whatever might hinder your prayer.

PRAY

Let the malice of the wicked come to an end, but sustain the just, O searcher of heart and soul, O just God.

~Psalm 7:10

LISTEN

Read John 7:40–53.

So a division occurred in the crowd because of him. Some of them even wanted to arrest him, but no one laid hands on him. So the guards went to the chief priests and Pharisees, who asked them, "Why did you not bring him?" The guards answered, "Never before has anyone spoken like this man."

~John 7:43–46

Who Is Responsible?

When Pope Francis made his first trip outside of Rome in July 2013, he visited the island of Lampedusa off the southern coast of Italy. Lampedusa is a kind of way station for people fleeing poverty and conflict in North Africa. Thousands have drowned trying to cross the Mediterranean, and the pope said he felt compelled to visit to show his solidarity with the migrants, mourn those who had been lost, and pose a blunt question.

"Who is responsible for the blood of these brothers and sisters of ours?" he asked in a homily. "Nobody!

That is our answer: It isn't me; I don't have anything to do with it; it must be someone else, but certainly not me. Yet God is asking each of us: 'Where is the blood of your brother which cries out to me?' Today no one in our world feels responsible; we have lost a sense of responsibility for our brothers and sisters."

Remarks such as these on the part of Pope Francis call to mind what the guards told the Pharisees and chief priests concerning Jesus: "Never before has anyone spoken like this man!" It's an apt analogy, because the pope is simply repeating what Jesus himself taught us: "Love one another." Perhaps the world had gotten so used to that message—and so used to disregarding it—that it is shocked to hear it repeated in such challenging terms. The least that can be said is that the world is listening to Pope Francis. It remains to be seen whether the world will respond with indifference. But we need not wait to answer for ourselves, and there is no better time than Lent.

ACT

I will seek a way as a volunteer or as a donor, or both, to directly serve the poor in my vicinity. I will include the poor in all of my prayers.

PRAY

You taught us that this is the whole law, to love God and to love all people as brothers and sisters. Help me to remember that to love as you love is to love without discrimination or condition. Help me to treat others' needs as though they were my own. Amen.

SUNDAY, MARCH 13
FIFTH WEEK OF LENT

BEGIN

Spend a minute or two in silence. Set aside whatever might hinder your prayer.

PRAY

Remember not the events of the past, the things of long ago consider not; see, I am doing something new! Now it springs forth, do you not perceive it? In the desert I make a way.

~Isaiah 43:18–19b

LISTEN

Read John 8:1–11.

But when they continued asking him, he straightened up and said to them, "Let the one among you who is without sin be the first to throw a stone at her." Again he bent down and wrote on the ground. And in response, they went away one by one, beginning with the elders.

~John 8:8–9a

"Has No One Condemned You?"

In his second inaugural address, Abraham Lincoln observed that people in both the North and the South read the same Bible and prayed to the same God, each invoking his aid against the other. He said, "It may seem strange that any men should dare to ask a just God's assistance in wringing their bread from the sweat of other men's faces; but let us judge not, that we be not judged."

Although the Civil War was about to end in a Union victory, Lincoln did not engage in the triumphalism that folks in the North might have expected. Slavery, he said, was "somehow the cause of the war," and he knew that the North was not blameless where slavery was concerned. Northerners had tolerated the "institution" as long as it was confined to states where it already existed, and Northern businesses—and therefore their customers and employees—had benefitted from it. Lincoln's balanced view of the conflict was a disappointment to those who looked forward to crushing the defeated South in retribution.

The men who brought an adulteress to Jesus were practicing a triumphalism of their own. The woman had sinned—there doesn't seem to be any doubt about that—and that justified their contempt, and they begged for her to be punished. Jesus embarrassed those men and gave a lesson to us all by reminding us that we all sin and we all need mercy and patience from God and from each other.

ACT

I will write on a card the names of two or three people whom I have judged harshly; I will keep the card with me throughout the day to remind me to say brief prayers for their well-being. I will make a point of greeting these people warmly when next I meet them.

PRAY

Merciful God, I have asked you again and again to forgive my sins. Now I pray for the clarity of vision to see that I share my weaknesses with others and that my duty is not to judge them but to treat them as brothers and sisters made, like me, in your image. Amen.

MONDAY, MARCH 14

FIFTH WEEK OF LENT

BEGIN

Spend a minute or two in silence. Set aside whatever might hinder your prayer.

PRAY

Only goodness and kindness follow me all the days of my life; and I shall dwell in the house of the LORD for years to come.

~*Psalm 23:6*

LISTEN

Read John 8:12–20.

Jesus spoke to them again, saying, "I am the light of the world. Whoever follows me will not walk in darkness, but will have the light of life."

~*John 8:12*

Disperse the Shadows

One of my favorite strips in the many *Peanuts* anthologies I have collected portrays a philosophical discussion between Charlie Brown and Lucy. Charlie Brown begins by asking if Lucy has ever considered what the world would be like if there were no sun. Yes, Lucy says, it's an intriguing question that can set the mind reeling: "This is the sort of proposition that can produce endless debate." And what, Charlie Brown asks, does Lucy herself think on this subject? Lucy answers, "It would be dark!"

Indeed, it would be because the sun is the source of virtually all natural light in our world. But the sun, in spite of its magnitude and power, is not the real light of the world. That, by his own testimony, is Jesus, who came to show human beings the path that leads to life forever with God—a path of love, charity, mercy, and justice. The Pharisees who heard Jesus describe himself this way were too intent on demeaning his teaching authority to understand that he was not aggrandizing himself but offering them and all people an intimate connection with a loving God. The Pharisees, as Jesus knew them, are gone from the scene, but many people in our own time still look everywhere except to Jesus for enlightenment. As Pope Francis has reminded us, we who are baptized have a vocation to carry the light of Christ to those people, wherever we find them, confidently testifying to our faith and bringing it to life in our service to others.

ACT

I will invite someone who has been away from the Church to attend one of the Easter Triduum liturgies with me next week. I will make my guest feel welcome in church and use the occasion to gently testify to the basis for my faith.

PRAY

Lord Jesus, you said that your followers would not walk in darkness. May I always walk only in the light of your Gospel and reflect that light for everyone I meet. Amen.

TUESDAY, MARCH 15
FIFTH WEEK OF LENT

BEGIN

Spend a minute or two in silence. Set aside whatever might hinder your prayer.

PRAY

The nations shall revere your name, O LORD, and all the kings of the earth your glory.

~Psalm 102:16

LISTEN

Read John 8:21–30.

So Jesus said to them, "When you lift up the Son of Man, then you will realize that I AM, and that I do nothing on my own, but I say only what the Father taught me."

~John 8:28

God and Man

In his 1983 movie *Zelig*, Woody Allen plays a man who is known as the "human chameleon." The nickname refers to the fact that the man, Leonard Zelig, so pines for acceptance that he takes on the physical characteristics and demeanors of the people around him—kitchen servants, party animals of the Roaring Twenties, and Nazis of prewar Germany. Allen tells the fictional story in the style of a documentary that portrays the attempts by a psychiatrist to raise Zelig's self-esteem so that he doesn't need to seek comfort in the identities of others.

Zelig portrays an absurdly extreme case of a real phenomenon that can occur with various degrees of severity—the lack of a strong sense of self or confusion about or discomfort with who a person is. In the passage from John's gospel, however, we meet a person whose sense of self could not be more clear. Our faith tells us what John's gospel expresses from its first verse: that Jesus is both God and man, that his ministry on earth is God's ministry on earth, and that his words are God's words. Jesus emphasizes his certainty about that every time he uses the expression "I AM," which scholars tell us alludes to a Hebrew term for God.

Although some skeptics try to dilute the identity of Jesus by conceding only that he was a wise teacher or an insightful prophet, we know better. The Jesus we encounter in his word, in the Eucharist, and in the quiet times of our Lenten practice shares our human nature and unites it intimately, inseparably, with the nature of God. Jesus knows who he is, and we are his disciples because we know too.

ACT

I will take time today to pray the Nicene Creed; I will pause after each phrase concerning the identity of Jesus, meditating on who he is, what he has done for me, and what I am called to do as his friend and disciple.

PRAY

Almighty God, by coming into the world in the person of Jesus you have demonstrated the depths of your love for us and shown us the value you place on the human person. Help me to imitate in my own humanity the example of holiness and compassion set by Jesus. Amen.

WEDNESDAY, MARCH 16
FIFTH WEEK OF LENT

BEGIN

*Spend a minute or two in silence. Set aside whatever
might hinder your prayer.*

PRAY

Blessed are you, O Lord, the God of our fathers,
praiseworthy and exalted above all forever; And
blessed is your holy and glorious name, praiseworthy and exalted above all for all ages.

~Daniel 3:52

LISTEN

Read John 8:31–42.

"I tell you what I have seen in the Father's presence; then do what you have heard from the
Father."

~John 8:38

"The Truth Will Set You Free"

In the 1951 musical *The King and I*, a nineteenth-cen-
tury king of Siam finds his equilibrium disrupted by
an English tutor he has hired to educate his children.
The teacher introduces ideas about personal freedom,
gender equality, and scientific inquiry foreign to the
closed society of Siam, and the king at first resists them.
He expresses his discomfiture, singing, "When I was a
boy, world was better spot. What was so was so, what
was not was not." But eventually the king, who wants
his country to be respected among the community of
nations, realizes that he cannot achieve his goal unless

he is willing to open himself and his people to the pursuit of truth.

The self-assurance that had kept the king in an archaic mindset provides a metaphor for the converts who debated with Jesus in the episode described in John's gospel. Those folks thought they were righteous just because they were "descendants of Abraham" and that they did not have to live up to the moral challenge Jesus was preaching. They wanted the security of being children of God without confronting the truth of what God expected of them.

In our own time, people can be misled by a similar self-assurance; they are so set on their autonomy that they see no need to measure their lives by the standard of the Gospel, which is the standard of submission to God's will and unselfish service to other human beings. May our Lenten observance recommit us to the generous, expansive life envisioned by the One who created us and not to a far more limited life we design for ourselves.

ACT

I will meditate on Jesus' command to "love one another" and experience the freedom of an unprovoked act of kindness or generosity.

PRAY

Lord Jesus Christ, you call us to escape the prison of self-absorption and live in the freedom of compassion and generosity. Help me to live the Gospel by imitating you, who showed us what it means to love one another. Amen.

THURSDAY, MARCH 17
FIFTH WEEK OF LENT

BEGIN

Spend a minute or two in silence. Set aside whatever might hinder your prayer.

PRAY

He remembers forever his covenant which he made binding for a thousand generations—which he entered into with Abraham.

~Psalm 105:8–9a

LISTEN

Read John 8:51–59.

Jesus said to them, "Amen, amen, I say to you, before Abraham came to be, I AM." So they picked up stones to throw at him; but Jesus hid and went out of the temple area.

~John 8:58–59

"Abraham Your Father Rejoiced"

Many years ago, a friend of mine, a rabbi, left his congregation to take up a hospital ministry in another state. I was one of twelve speakers at a farewell program at his synagogue. My family attended, and our kids, who knew nothing of this or any other rabbi, sat quietly through the testimonials. But after the program had concluded and the rabbi walked over to greet us, my preteen daughters—after hearing about his impact on individuals and a whole community—both rushed up to him and hugged him as though he were an uncle or grandfather.

That scene—Christian children embracing a Jewish elder—is a helpful image to keep in mind in these next few days when we hear so much in the gospels about "the Jews" persecuting Jesus. The first reading at today's Mass (Gn 17:3–9) is the account of God's covenant with Abraham, the father of the Jewish people, and his descendants, a covenant that God says—and the Catholic Church teaches—will last until the end of time. And as Jesus implies in the gospel passage, the Jewish faith was the tree from which the Christian faith took root and flourished. The fact that certain religious leaders were antagonistic toward Jesus and wanted to stifle him in no way impugns Judaism itself or all Jewish people then or now.

Gospel passages we will read between now and Good Friday have been carelessly or deliberately misconstrued so as to justify unspeakable atrocities against Jews. As we contemplate the passion of Jesus, let us also contemplate the passion of the people from whom he was born to be the savior of the world.

ACT

I will read Genesis 17:3–9 and pray for the safety and well-being of Jewish people everywhere.

PRAY

Almighty God, may hatred for the Jewish people be eradicated from the minds of human beings. Regardless of our faith, may our love for you and our love for each other be the only motivation for our actions. We ask this through Jesus Christ, our Lord. Amen.

FRIDAY, MARCH 18
FIFTH WEEK OF LENT

BEGIN

Spend a minute or two in silence. Set aside whatever might hinder your prayer.

PRAY

I love you, O LORD, my strength, O LORD, my rock, my fortress, my deliverer.

~Psalm 18:2–3a

LISTEN

Read John 10:31–42.

"If I do not perform my Father's works, do not believe me; but if I perform them, even if you do not believe me, believe the works, so that you may realize and understand that the Father is in me and I am in the Father."

~John 10:37–38

About the Father's Business

A small gaggle of customers in my family's grocery store were killing part of a Saturday morning by gossiping about our pastor. According to the chatter, the priest was undignified, abrupt, cheap, obese, and obsessed with fundraising. When the merry party had dispersed, a man who worked for my family muttered to me, "When he's gone, they'll erect a statue of him and swear he was a saint."

It didn't work out exactly that way—there was no statue—but fifty years later I still hear people speak highly of him. He served the parish for twenty-five years. During that time, he built a rectory, a new church, and a convent, and he converted the old church into the town's first Catholic school. When I say "he built," I don't mean it figuratively. He swept, shoveled, swung a hammer, wielded a wrecking bar, and spread concrete in spite of an advanced case of arthritis. He celebrated liturgies with care and preached with energy; he was accessible, good-natured, and friendly.

When Father died, our bishop said in the funeral homily that diocesan records showed that our pastor had less personal wealth when he retired than he did when he emerged from the seminary. Clearly, Father was interested in only one thing—doing God's works. He had his model in Jesus, who did God's works despite indifference, criticism, and threats to his life. We shouldn't let Lent slip away without asking ourselves how well we imitate that model; it was meant for us, too.

ACT

Before Easter Sunday, I will do something that is clearly the Father's work: directly aid the poor, bring gifts to a nursing home, visit an elderly person who lives alone, or ask my pastor what task most badly needs doing in the parish.

PRAY

Lord Jesus, you asked your persecutors to judge you based on whether you did the works of the Father. May I be measured by the same standard, and may I be judged a faithful servant. Amen.

Saturday, March 19
St. Joseph, Husband of the Blessed Virgin Mary

BEGIN

Spend a minute or two in silence. Set aside whatever might hinder your prayer.

PRAY

The promises of the LORD I will sing forever; through all generations my mouth shall proclaim your faithfulness, for you have said, "My kindness is established forever"; in heaven you have confirmed your faithfulness.

Psalm 89:2–3

LISTEN

Read Matthew 1:16, 18–21, 24a.

When Joseph awoke, he did as the angel of the Lord had commanded him and took his wife into his home.

~Matthew 1:24a

An Unknown Model

One characteristic of the scriptures that frustrates many readers is that the authors provide so few details about most of the personalities they write about. In the gospels, for instance, many would like to know more about the magi, Simeon and Anna, the individual apostles, Lazarus, or the wife of Pontius Pilate. Certainly many would like to know more about Joseph, the husband of Mary. The solemnity we celebrate today, even during Lent, indicates the esteem in which the Church holds

Joseph. But the Gospel of Mark doesn't mention him at all and the Gospel of John mentions him only in passing. We never hear him speak. All we know about him is contained in relatively few passages in the Gospels of Matthew and Luke, and we know nothing of him from the time Jesus was twelve years old.

But the evangelists were not writing biography; they were writing the story of our salvation. They told us about Joseph only what they thought we needed to know. What we need to know is that Joseph was a devout man who observed the Law of God, that he was a just man whose only goal was to shield Mary from disgrace when he learned she was pregnant, that he was a faithful man who submitted to what he understood to be God's will, and that he was a courageous and responsible man who took care of his family under the most difficult circumstances. We know enough to see Joseph as our model and to do our best to imitate his qualities, keeping faith with God as we navigate the twists and turns in our own lives.

ACT

I will spend time reflecting on decisions I make in everyday life and major decisions I may have to make in the foreseeable future. I will ask the Holy Spirit to help me understand God's will before I make any significant choice.

PRAY

Almighty God, you chose Joseph as the guardian of Jesus and his mother, Mary. Help me, like Joseph, to always see clearly the role you have chosen for me and to carry it out according to your will. Amen.

Sunday, March 20

Palm Sunday of the Lord's Passion

BEGIN

Spend a minute or two in silence. Set aside whatever might hinder your prayer.

PRAY

I will proclaim your name to my brethren; in the midst of the assembly I will praise you: "You who fear the Lord, praise him; all you descendants of Jacob, give glory to him; revere him, all you descendants of Israel!"

~Psalm 22:23–24

LISTEN

Read Luke 22:14–23:56.

"I am among you as the one who serves. It is you who have stood by me in my trials; and I confer a kingdom on you, just as my Father has conferred one on me, that you may eat and drink at my table in my kingdom."

~Luke 22:27b–30a

Take Up Your Cross

Cardinal Donald Wuerl began a Palm Sunday homily by telling a story about himself. Cardinal Wuerl said that he had found himself at a fund-raising event standing near a teenaged boy who had a spinal disorder that made it impossible for him to stand unaided. He was using two handheld crutches. A woman, who seemingly meant well, told the teenager that he was "a brave young man," to which the boy replied, "Lady, everybody has a cross to bear. You can just see mine."

The teenager was right: everybody has a cross, or more than one, and the burden can take many forms. Some folks are chronically ill or physically challenged, some have emotional or psychological issues, some have addictions, some have financial struggles, some are lonely, and some experience regular work problems.

We are human beings and, clerk or cardinal, our existence is limited. During this Holy Week, we recall that when God took on human form in the person of Jesus, he took on the reality of the Cross, accepting even violent death. But as Jesus repeatedly implied, the Cross he willingly carried would not be the end for him. It would be the gateway to glory.

Jesus carried the Cross in solidarity with us, and he calls on us to bear our burdens in solidarity with him, still faithful to his commandments of service and love, still confident that we will live beyond our crosses and be with him in paradise.

ACT

I will pray that God will relieve others whose burdens are greater than my own and ask him to inspire me to live as Jesus did, as a servant to others, regardless of the crosses I carry.

PRAY

Lord Jesus, I want to model my life after yours, accepting with grace any obstacles I encounter and using what energy and resources I have to bless the lives of my neighbors as I wait to be with you forever in heaven. Amen.

Monday, March 21
Holy Week

BEGIN

Spend a minute or two in silence. Set aside whatever might hinder your prayer.

PRAY

The LORD is my light and my salvation; whom should I fear? The LORD is my life's refuge; of whom should I be afraid?

~Psalm 27:1

LISTEN

Read John 12:1–11.

"You always have the poor with you, but you do not always have me."

~John 12:8

"Where Your Treasure Is"

In 2005, ten bottles of Clive Christian No. 1 perfume were offered for sale. One 16.9-ounce bottle, adorned with diamonds and 18-carat gold, was priced at $205,000.

The value of perfume is ultimately determined by what someone is willing to pay for it. Judas implied that the perfumed oil Mary used to anoint Jesus was worth three hundred days' wages. He might have been exaggerating, but the gospel describes the oil as "costly," and that is all we need to know. It tells us that Mary was willing to pay a high price because of the value she placed on Jesus, who had taught her the

Good News and raised her brother, Lazarus, to new life.

When Judas complained that the oil should have been sold to raise money for the poor, Jesus gave a paradoxical answer: "You always have the poor with you, but you do not always have me." It sounds as if Jesus were making himself more important than the poor, contradicting his own teaching. But this remark was addressed to Judas, and the writer tells us that Judas didn't care about the poor; he cared only about enriching himself and was willing to sell even Jesus himself. In Matthew's gospel, Jesus tells us, "Where your treasure is, there also will your heart be." If we—like Mary and unlike poor Judas—value the presence of Jesus in our lives and put his teaching into practice, then we will also value the poor and do everything we can to help them.

ACT

I will write a letter to myself, honestly listing the things in life that are of greatest value to me and the things in life that occupy most of my time, energy, and material resources. I will pray about whether I am satisfied with these lists and, if not, what I can do to reorder them.

PRAY

Almighty God, you have given us existence itself, life, an immortal soul, and the ministry and sacrifice of your Son, Jesus Christ. Help me to value these gifts above all things and to show my gratitude by being a gift to others in my everyday life. Amen.

TUESDAY, MARCH 22
HOLY WEEK

BEGIN

Spend a minute or two in silence. Set aside whatever might hinder your prayer.

PRAY

In you, O LORD, I take refuge; let me never be put to shame. In your justice rescue me, and deliver me; incline your ear to me, and save me.

~Psalm 71:1–2

LISTEN

Read John 13:21–33, 36–38.

After Judas took the morsel, Satan entered him. So Jesus said to him, "What you are going to do, do quickly." . . . So Judas took the morsel and left at once. And it was night.

~John 12:27, 30

The Reach of God's Mercy

The 1936 movie *Prisoner of Shark Island* tells the story of Dr. Samuel Mudd, convicted of conspiracy in the murder of Abraham Lincoln. In this film, a guard at the island fortress where Mudd is incarcerated calls the doctor "Judas." The guard doesn't have to explain himself. Anyone who hears that name knows what it implies. Judas Iscariot is the poster boy for betrayal— he betrayed the savior of the world, after all—and Christian society subjects him to a level of revulsion that it applies to few people.

This unenviable status that Judas has achieved raises a question: Has he sunk so low that God would not forgive him? The answer may seem obvious considering what Judas did, but in fact, it is beyond our competence to decide as it would be with respect to anyone else. We don't know anything about the interior life of Judas. We can't reconstruct his past, we can't know what was going on in his mind, and we can't know that he is beyond the reach of God's mercy. In fact, we can pray for his redemption just as we can pray for other people who have offended us and just as we can pray for ourselves when we fall short of being images of Christ in this world.

Pope Francis has stressed throughout his papacy that God's mercy is inexhaustible and that ours should be as well. If we want mercy for ourselves, we can ask it even for someone like Judas, who is, after all, our brother.

ACT

I will ask myself whom in my own life it is time to forgive. I will pray for God's mercy on all of us who have sinned and ask him to lift from my heart the weight of my judgment of others.

PRAY

Merciful God, you alone can read the human heart; you alone know what moves us to act as we do. Thank you for your eagerness to forgive even the greatest of sinners. Give me the grace to bring my own sorrow and regrets to you, to sincerely repent my sins, and to gratefully accept your forgiveness. Amen.

WEDNESDAY, MARCH 23
HOLY WEEK

BEGIN

Spend a minute or two in silence. Set aside whatever might hinder your prayer.

PRAY

See, the Lord GOD is my help; who will prove me wrong?

~*Isaiah 50:9a*

LISTEN

Read Matthew 26:14–25.

When it was evening, he reclined at table with the Twelve. And while they were eating, he said, "Amen, I say to you, one of you will betray me." Deeply distressed at this, they began to say to him one after another, "Surely it is not I, Lord?"

~*Matthew 26:20–22*

"I Call You My Friends"

Most of us have probably heard the Latin phrase *Et tu, Brute?* meaning, "And you, Brutus?" The phrase was made famous by William Shakespeare in his play *Julius Caesar*. It is uttered by Caesar when he sees among his assassins Marcus Junius Brutus, who he had thought was his friend. Shakespeare wasn't the first Elizabethan to use this phrase, but ancient historians reported that Caesar said nothing when he was set upon by men bound to prevent him from becoming ruler of Rome for life.

Although the remark is fictional, it expresses a plaintive sentiment, the dismay after being betrayed by someone close. Jesus, in his human nature, no doubt experienced that feeling when Judas turned against him after having heard the Good News. And although we don't fully understand the glorified Christ, we might imagine that he feels that twinge of pain whenever any one of us, having heard the Gospel, fails to carry it out in our lives. Tomorrow we begin our commemoration of the events in which Christ sealed his covenant with us by giving himself to us, first in the Eucharist and then on the Cross. It was a lot to give, but he loved us—his friends—that much. We don't always return that love. Perhaps it would help us as we make the many decisions that direct our daily lives to keep before us the image of Jesus asking, "And you?"

ACT

I will read one of the gospel accounts of the crucifixion and death of Jesus, meditate on the depth of his love for me, and pray a fervent act of contrition.

PRAY

Lord Jesus, you gave your life for me and for all so that we might live together with God in eternity. If my friendship for you is imperfect, if I betray you at times, accept my contrition and my determination to always return to your side when I have wandered. Amen.

THE EASTER TRIDUUM

On these days, it is important to pray together with your parish community. These meditations are brief so that you may spend time participating in the Church's most sacred liturgies.

APRIL 24

HOLY THURSDAY

LISTEN

Read John 13:1–15.

> So when he had washed their feet and put his garments back on and reclined at table again, he said to them, "Do you realize what I have done for you? You call me 'teacher' and 'master,' and rightly so, for indeed I am. If I, therefore, the master and teacher, have washed your feet, you ought to wash one another's feet. I have given you a model to follow, so that as I have done for you, you should also do."

> *~John 13:12–15*

"In Remembrance of Me"

On my dresser is a coin bank, a miniature building, that belonged to my father. In the coin bank are about two dozen dimes that have been handled so much that the images on them are almost worn away. Dad kept this bank with its "thin dimes" on his own dresser, and it is for me an important memento of him.

We cherish such things to remember our loved ones by, and on this day we celebrate the remembrance par excellence—the Eucharist. The passage from St. Paul's first letter to the Corinthians that is read in the liturgy this evening is the oldest account of the Last Supper—dating to at least AD 54. The words, recorded close to the event itself, are repeated at every Mass. Everyone who comes to that Eucharistic meal is called not only to remember Jesus but also to imitate him, to imitate the example of unselfish service he performed when he washed the feet of his apostles. Jesus asked us to remember and to *be* him in the lives of those who need us.

PRAY

> Lord Jesus, you have given us the greatest remembrance of all—the gift of yourself in the Eucharist. May I always give thanks for that gift by living as you lived, a life of compassion and service. Amen.

APRIL 25

GOOD FRIDAY

LISTEN

Read John 18:1–19:42.

> After this, aware that everything was now finished, in order that the Scripture might be fulfilled, Jesus said, "I thirst." There was a vessel filled with common wine. So they put a sponge soaked in wine on a sprig of hyssop and put it up to his mouth. When Jesus had taken the wine, he said, "It is finished." And bowing his head, he handed over the spirit.
>
> ~*John 19:28–30*

By Your Holy Cross You Have Redeemed Us

Sam M. Lewis was a prolific songwriter. Many of his lyrics have been forgotten; others are standards. But

Lewis's most poignant song was "I Heard a Forest Praying." Lewis wrote that trees provide a play area for children, conceal a lovers' lane, and "shelter the tired and the weary." But then the lyrics note that humans have also turned fields and forests into battlefields, and "Men took a tree—an innocent tree—and made a cross for him." Lewis didn't have to mention Jesus' name. We know that the Cross that arrests our attention today was the "tree" on which Jesus died. We need to recall that his death was the consequence of sin and that sin continues to cause him pain. But we also need to recall that, regardless of the motives of the men who made that Cross, the only motive Jesus had for submitting to it was his inexhaustible love for us. He died in order to rise. He died so that we might rise with him. That's why, on this Good Friday, we kiss the Cross.

PRAY

> Lord Jesus, I recall with deep regret the pain you suffered out of love for us. May the image of your Cross keep me from ever hurting you, and may it inspire me to give unselfishly of myself and be a source of new life to others. Amen.

APRIL 26

HOLY SATURDAY

LISTEN

Read Luke 24:1–12.

"Why do you seek the living one among the dead? He is not here, but he has been raised. Remember what he said to you while he was still in Galilee,

that the Son of Man must be handed over to sinners
and be crucified, and rise on the third day."

~Luke 24:5b–7

The World Awaits Its Savior

Something strange is happening—there is a great
silence on earth today, a great silence and stillness. The
whole earth keeps silence because the King is asleep.
The earth trembled and is still because God has fallen
asleep in the flesh and he has raised up all who have
slept ever since the world began.

That is from an ancient homily that is included in
the Office of Readings in the Liturgy of the Hours for
this day. It refers to the Church's teaching that after his
death Jesus visited the souls denied access to heaven
since the sin of Adam, assuring them that redemption was at hand. During this time, according to the
homily, the world waited breathlessly for what was to
follow—resurrection!

The world on this Saturday is probably not still at
all. Much of the world on this Saturday is probably not
anticipating the Resurrection but is busy with something else. But we can create that stillness for ourselves,
taking the time to absorb the enormity of what God has
done for us and what he has promised to do—restore
us to new life no matter how often we may die in sin.

PRAY

Almighty God, you so loved the world that you
gave up your only Son to death so that we might
share with you eternal life. May I always see my
own desires and concerns in the light of this sacrifice. Amen.

APRIL 27
EASTER SUNDAY

LISTEN

Read Acts 10:34a, 37–43.

"He commissioned us to preach to the people and testify that he is the one appointed by God as judge of the living and the dead. To him all the prophets bear witness, that everyone who believes in him will receive forgiveness of sins through his name."

~Acts 10:42–43